"All Christians believe in the Trinity, but most Christians, if we're honest, don't like to think about the Trinity that much. The doctrine seems abstract, dry, and distant from everyday life. This book will change that for you. Joe Thorn points us to the joy of a God who is Father, Son, and Spirit, showing us how this truth should prompt us to worship, pray, and trust. He applies this great doctrine without putting us out of its mystery. This book can better equip you to praise the God from whom all blessings flow."

Russell D. Moore, President, The Ethics & Religious Liberty Commission; author, *Tempted and Tried*

"*Experiencing the Trinity* will help us focus on God in the midst of the dark clouds and thundering waves that threaten to sink us. The book you hold now is short, but the truths contained therein are neither flippant nor light. It's just the kind of ballast you need in life's storms."

Gloria Furman, Pastor's wife, Redeemer Church of Dubai; mother of four; author, *Glimpses of Grace* and *Treasuring Christ When Your Hands Are Full*

"Here's gospel gold emerging from the furnace of affliction. Truth that's been lived becomes life giving as Joe comforts others with the comfort with which he has been comforted by God. I hope and pray that these beautiful meditations will do you as much good as they did me."

David P. Murray, Professor of Old Testament and Practical Theology, Puritan Reformed Theological Seminary

EXPERIENCING THE TRINITY

———————————

EXPERIENCING

—— THE ——

TRINITY

THE GRACE OF GOD
FOR THE PEOPLE OF GOD

JOE THORN

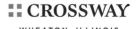

:: CROSSWAY

WHEATON, ILLINOIS

Trade paperback ISBN: 978-1-4335-4168-1
ePub ISBN: 978-1-4335-4171-1
PDF ISBN: 978-1-4335-4169-8
Mobipocket ISBN: 978-1-4335-4170-4

Library of Congress Cataloging-in-Publication Data

Thorn, Joe, 1972–
   Experiencing the Trinity : the grace of God for the people of God / Joe Thorn.
      pages cm
   Includes bibliographical references.
   ISBN 978-1-4335-4168-1 (tp)
   1. Trinity—Meditations. I. Title.
BT111.3.T46   2015
231'.044 — dc23   2014029750

Crossway is a publishing ministry of Good News Publishers.

LB		25	24	23	22	21	20	19	18	17	16	15
15	14	13	12	11	10	9	8	7	6	5	4	3	2	1

To

Katherine, Elias, Madeline, and Kilian.
May you always know the love and grace
of our triune God.

Contents

Part 2   God the Son

Part 3　God the Holy Spirit

Introduction

I am intending to speak to none but myself,
and therefore shall only observe what is useful
to my own heart and practice.[1]

Richard Baxter

What I have written here, I have primarily written for and to myself. I needed to hear these words during a desperate period of my life, and though that particular time of affliction has passed, I continue to need them today. I hope that these reflections on the grace of our triune God will encourage those who find themselves battling fear, anxiety, temptation, affliction, and doubt. I am there with you, but more importantly, so is the Lord.

The Dark Night of My Soul

In 2011, shortly after the publication of my first book, *Note to Self*, I started to fall apart. While walking down

---

[1] Richard Baxter, *Dying Thoughts* (Edinburgh, UK: Banner of Truth Trust, 2004), 2.

Wabash Avenue in Chicago my hands began to shake, and I grew exceedingly fearful. This sense of dread came upon me suddenly and did not abate, and I had to make it through one more appointment. I made it through that meeting by sitting on my hands and wearing my best poker face. Immediately after the appointment I called my wife to tell her what I was experiencing. On the train ride home I prayed a lot, knowing I was heading into something painful.

This was the beginning of the most difficult season in my personal life. My marriage and family were healthy and our church was vital and growing, yet I felt like I was withering and dying. I lost every form of confidence I had in the things God had called me to do and was oppressed by an abiding sense of fear and deep anxiety. Regular and easy meetings with people in the congregation left me terribly anxious, and regardless of how pleasant or successful they were, I left each meeting feeling like a failure. I experienced little sleep during this time. I began doubting my calling, and was afraid that I would not be able to lead the church into its next stage of life.

For the first time in my life I was the weakest man I knew. I was truly frail. This led me to cry out to the Lord and "preach to myself" more than any other time. Yet relief was often slow in coming. I would pour over pages of Scripture and lie face down waiting for God to refresh my heart, assure my soul, and lift my head. Sometimes I was blessed with peace, other times I was left in my condition. It was as if I were walking in darkness and afraid of falling off a cliff, and although the promise of light was given, I was still waiting for it to break through the night.

The Way Out of Darkness

A friend told me to reach out to Dr. David Murray, professor of Old Testament and Practical Theology at Puritan Reformed Theological Seminary in Grand Rapids, Michigan. I was surprised to find out he had read my book and had an idea of who I was. As we talked, he asked me dozens of questions to get a better understanding of what I was going through and what my habits were. Over the next several months David became a lifeline of wisdom and a friend for whom I am forever grateful. God led me out of the darkness through my family, my church, my friends, my doctor, and especially Dr. Murray.

The simplest way to explain how I wound up in such trouble is to say that I had been working too hard for too long without resting. Some people call it burnout. My body and soul were suffering, and things needed to change. I had to delegate a number of responsibilities, adjust my sleep habits, take Sabbath rest seriously, and restructure my schedule—all while maintaining communion with Christ through prayer and the Word. With these changes I experienced some relief, but still woke up in the middle of the night with heart palpitations, and much of my fear remained with me. After consulting with Dr. Murray and my physician I began taking medication for anxiety.

Taking prescription drugs for my mental health had never before been an option. I saw all of my battles as only spiritual, with no real physical component. I wanted to trust God and experience his deliverance, but in the midst of my praying, repenting, believing, and pouring over the Word of God, relief was slow in coming. Dr. Murray helped me to think through this biblically and theologically. On his recommendation, I read Richard Baxter's *The Cure of Melancholy and Overmuch Sorrow by Faith and Physic*. I was surprised to find that the well-known Puritan argued that medicine is sometimes needed in the cure of those suffering from what we now call mental illness. Baxter explains:

> If other means will not do, neglect not physic [medicine]; and though they will be averse to it, as believing that the disease is only in the mind, they must be persuaded or forced to it. I have known the lady deep in melancholy, who a long time would neither

speak, nor take physic, nor endure her husband to
go out of the room, and with the restraint and grief
he died, and she was cured by physic put down her
throat with a pipe by force.[2]

No one had to get out a pipe, but it took quite a bit
of time and prayer before I was willing to seriously consider the idea that my brain wasn't functioning properly and that medicine might be a critical part of my
journey toward health. In fact, it was.

Of course, medicine alone didn't fix me. A new schedule didn't really free me. God used a number of changes
that worked together to rebuild me. And central to it
all was the Word of God. It was Scripture that drew me
back to the hope, peace, and safety I have in Jesus. And
that is what this book is really about: how the Word of
God draws us to the living God. In knowing him we find
peace, joy, strength, and faith.

Yet the power of God's Word is not seen in the im-
mediacy of its work. Preaching God's Word to yourself
is not necessarily a quick fix for your sorrows and suffering. At times God will delay granting you relief in
order to draw you closer to himself. He might want to
teach you just how helpless you really are and how all-
sufficient he really is. Sometimes God will allow you to

---

[2] Richard Baxter, *The Cure of Melancholy and Overmuch Sorrow by Faith and Physic* in *The Practical Works of the Rev. Richard Baxter,* vol. 17 (London: James Duncan, 1830). Kindle edition.

suffer for a season to test and strengthen your faith. I am thankful that I have learned that belief is easy when life is easy, but when life is confusing and painful, faith will prove itself to be either rooted in Jesus Christ or resting on religious sentiments.

I can now praise the Lord for his delay of peace, for it not only tested my faith, but made the grace he finally did give that much sweeter.

Notes to Myself

What follows are fifty daily readings that reflect on God and the gospel and how they overcome our fear, failure, pain, and unbelief. Much of this I preached to myself over the last couple of years, and all of it is directed toward my own heart. So, for instance, when I write "there is a kind of deficiency in your christology," I'm referring primarily to my own weakness. But if you find yourself with a heart like mine, weak and in need of grace, I pray these readings will be an encouragement to you. For God offers his grace to people like us.

> He has pity on the weak and the needy,
>   and saves the lives of the needy. (Ps. 72:13)

But allow me to be clear from the start. As this little book is written to myself, it comes from the perspective of a Christian and it is written to a Christian. If you have not yet believed in Jesus Christ as the only hope of being reconciled to God, I encourage you to read the following pages as the promises God makes to those who believe. Until you believe in Jesus, these promises remain only a potential reality for you. They are not yet yours, but they are offered to you. You must receive them by trusting in Jesus Christ yourself. Believing in Jesus is not choosing a new religion, but seeing your own sin and just condemnation before God. It is awaking to your idolatry and seeing the worthiness of the one true God. Trusting in Jesus means believing that your only hope to stand before the face of God and experience mercy is found in the life, death, and resurrection of his Son.

What I hope you will discover—what I continue to learn over and over again—is that all of us are far weaker than we know. Our sin, which is much darker and goes much deeper than we realize, is the real source of our most significant weakness. Neither you nor I can measure up to God's standards. We are trapped in our condition of guilt, and the only hope is the offer of grace by our triune God.

Part 1

GOD THE FATHER

1

He Is Holy

Holy, holy, holy is the Lᴏʀᴅ of hosts;
the whole earth is full of his glory!

Isaiah 6:3

You don't have an Isaiah 6 experience with God very
often. I'm not referring to prophetic visions; I'm talking
about having an encounter with God as *holy*. I mean an
intense and transformative interaction with the Lord
who dwells in unapproachable light—the kind of experience that drops you to your knees in the fear of
God and moves you to confess your sins. Do you even
remember the last time you said, "Woe is me"? Have
you ever said it?

Despite the books, sermons, and songs that high-
light the holiness of God, this doctrine remains too in-
frequently on your mind, and it insufficiently informs
how you approach and live for God. It's not enough that

you properly define God's holiness. Reading Dr. Sproul's classic treatment of the subject is wonderful, but this central aspect of God's character must also be experienced.[1] The less you are gripped with God's holiness, the less awe you will experience in your faith. A truer sight of his holiness will give you a truer sight of your corruptions. And it is only as you see both of these realities that you will find his mercy extended toward you in Jesus Christ to be soul-satisfying and worship-inspiring.

Awe of God proceeds from knowing and experiencing his holiness—his *otherness*. He is unlike people in many ways. He is high and lifted up in his sovereignty, justice, and goodness. He is pure. There is no darkness in the Lord. He is perfect in every way. To see even a vision of him, as Isaiah did, makes your legs weak and jaw drop. And if all you saw were his holiness in contrast to your sinfulness, you would despair and lose all hope of living before him.

But the holiness of God includes his mercy and grace. He is not only the Lord of justice, but also the Lord of compassion. He cleanses the filthy and pardons the guilty. He purifies his people and clothes them in the righteousness of his Son, Jesus, making them acceptable in his presence. The holiness of God lifts the soul in worship, for holiness is the sum of all he is.

---

[1] R. C. Sproul, *The Holiness of God* (Carol Stream, IL: Tyndale, 2001).

Look to your holy God. Behold his glory. He is more than you can comprehend, and what he has shown you of himself is enough to forever change you. Behold his glory. The whole earth is full of it, but does his glory fill your mind and heart?

He Is Creator

The LORD is the everlasting God,
  the Creator of the ends of the earth.

Isaiah 40:28

That God created the heavens and the earth is one of the most important doctrines revealed in the Bible. It's a shame you seldom think so. God as Creator is not throwaway theology. It isn't just teaching for the kids. Yes, it's critical Sunday school instruction, but the church gives it to young people early so that they will hold on to it throughout their lives. To say God is Creator is to say he is the one in whom you find your identity and purpose.

Your God has not only created the world, but he has also created you. You exist because God chose to make you. And when he made you, he made you for himself. Meditate on this. You were made for your Maker's pleasure. You are here for the sake of Another. And this doesn't diminish your purpose or value in life. In fact, it heightens it. It's counterintuitive, I know, but stop listening to the world for a minute.

One of the lies the world continually presents is that you are not only in control, but that you indeed are your own master. You say to yourself, "I am the master of my fate, I am the captain of my soul."[1] It makes for interesting poetry, but it also makes for a life that will fail in the most significant ways.

You did not create yourself, and you cannot re-create yourself. Your value is not found in your uniqueness or your individuality. It is found in the God who created you in his own image. Yes, you are special, *sacred* really, but this is because you, in amazing ways, look like the God who made you. And this is not your uniqueness. In fact this is what makes you common—like every other person on earth. You were made by God, for God.

Sadly, you do not live the life your Creator intended. You have often attempted to set the course of your life as if you were the captain. Such rebellion is what mars the image of God. You were created for a person and with a purpose, but you have often worked to undo much of that. But do not despair. The God who creates also re-creates. He has caused you to be born again.

---

[1] William Ernest Henley, *Invictus,* 1888.

He has given you a new heart. He has made you something new.

> Therefore, if anyone is in Christ, he is a new creation. The old has passed away; behold, the new has come. (2 Cor. 5:17)

To know God as Creator is to recognize that you are his creature. As a Christian you are doubly his, for he has made you and remade you for his glory. You truly are his workmanship.

He Is Powerful

Our God is in the heavens;
    he does all that he pleases.

Psalm 115:3

You often feel powerless. At times, your weakness and frailty overtake you so that you lose hope. It wouldn't matter so much if you weren't in situations that demanded power, performance, and perseverance, but that is exactly where you find yourself. You need to do something, and you cannot do it. Such powerlessness, such inability, is not only discouraging but also defeating. Take this to heart: you are weak, but your God is not.

God is absolutely sovereign, having all power and controlling all things. He can do as he pleases—and he does. To say that God is sovereign is one thing. You say it often. But to *know* that your God is sovereign should be a great encouragement to your soul when you face what looks to be impossible.

Consider your great enemies. The world, the flesh, the Devil, and death. They are terrible foes, yet God is sovereign over them and has overcome each one through the work of his Son Jesus Christ. Consider the calling with which you have been called: believe in Jesus; take up your cross and follow him; forgive your enemies; give generously; be content with what you have. This and so much more of what you are called to do is simply too much. Own that. You *cannot* do it. Not on your own. But you are not alone. Your God is with you, and until you embrace your weakness, you will never experience his power.

Those who are in Christ are brought near to God and know his power. He has given you his Spirit who comes upon you with power to bear witness to the Savior (Acts 1:8). God has given you a spirit of power, love, and self-control (2 Tim. 1:7). He gives you grace in the midst of your weakness to make his sovereign care known (2 Cor. 12:9). God guards you and guides you in such a way that you are empowered to persevere (1 Pet. 1:5). And God's sovereign power is at work in weak people like you when you pray—when you seek his help in your time of need (James 5:16).

Yes, you are weak, but the sovereign God of the universe is with you. The Holy Spirit is in you. Jesus himself says that he is ever with you. Whatever towers before you is small before your all-powerful God.

4

He Is Present

Fear not, for I am with you;
  be not dismayed, for I am your God;
I will strengthen you, I will help you,
  I will uphold you with my righteous
    right hand.

Isaiah 41:10

God is *omnipresent*. This attribute is an essential part of his being as the eternal God who fills all time and space. But there is a great difference to God being everywhere and God being with you. It is this latter truth that will conquer your anxieties and comfort you in your loneliness.

God's presence in your life is one of the great gospel promises given throughout Scripture. God has always held this truth out as one of the great blessings of being reconciled to him: "The LORD your God is in your midst"

(Zeph. 3:17); "I will make my dwelling among you, and my soul shall not abhor you. And I will walk among you and will be your God, and you shall be my people" (Lev. 26:11–12). Jesus ended his earthly ministry with this promise: "Behold, I am with you always" (Matt. 28:20). With such promises, why are you so often going at life as if you are alone?

Sure, there are times when you face something alone—when friends are gone and you cannot find help from a brother or sister. But the absence of a worldly companion does not leave you without hope or help. For even when you walk through the valley of the shadow of death, God is with you to protect you, strengthen you, and accomplish his good purposes through you. You are never really alone, but unless you are seeking communion with the Lord who is there, you will feel alone. You will carry the burden. And in doing so you will remain afraid and collapse under the weight of your afflictions.

Rest in the reality of God's presence. If God is with his people, then as a Christian you can rest assured that he is with you. And if God is with you, to uphold you, you have the promise of perseverance. The presence of God the Father will grant you rest and hope in the midst of all things that drive fear into the hearts of men and women.

He Provides

Look at the birds of the air: they neither sow nor reap nor gather into barns, and yet your heavenly Father feeds them. Are you not of more value than they?

Matthew 6:26

The Lord is a God of providence. He governs all things and is intimately involved in all that happens in the world. This means that he is "all in" when it comes to the details of your life. There is never a moment of your day when God is inactive. He is there and he is involved. The grace of God abounds to those who have trusted in Jesus Christ, and his providential and spiritual care of you guarantees that all of your needs will be met.

The uncertainties of life, the accompanying worries connected to the what-ifs, can be settled in this great truth: come what may, God will never leave you or forsake you. Rather, he promises to supply you with whatever you need in this life and in the life to come.

I know your mind goes quickly to those believers who have starved to death or who suffered great and unjust affliction. You wonder, "How did God provide for them?" But that question reveals that your understanding of what is *needed* is far narrower than what God knows is needed and best. He will provide, but you can miss his provision if you're waiting for him to give only what you are looking for.

To say that God will always provide for you is not to say that he will give you every earthly thing you desire. It's not a guarantee that you will receive what you need for a long and comfortable life on earth. It is the guarantee that wherever you are, God remains present; that whatever you go through, God has a sovereign purpose; and that whatever your affliction or difficulty, God will provide you with the grace you need to persevere in faith and find satisfaction in him. God provides what is best, and sometimes what is best is that which you would never choose. Sometimes that which is painful for a time will yield a greater blessing later, even if you must wait for it until after death.

6

He Is Good

Good and upright is the LORD;
> therefore he instructs sinners
>> in the way.
He leads the humble in what is right,
> and teaches the humble his way.

Psalm 25:8–9

The doctrine of God's goodness is at the heart of some of your struggles. You affirm that God is sovereign and present, but you still fear and doubt his goodness. God is good, which means that he always does what is right; this stems from his very character. He is not good according to the standards of man. He is far better than that. He is trustworthy.

Because God is who he is, you can trust him in all things at all times. He is good and upright, and he instructs sinners in the Way. Do you see that? He instructs *sinners*. He doesn't abandon them, but he teaches them. Such an education is often painful. He convicts his children of sin; he afflicts their consciences that they may better see the ugliness of their corruption. But he does this with care and from a caring heart. It is his goodness that moves him to care for them in these ways.

Understanding that God is absolutely sovereign will do you little good if you do not also understand his goodness. He is not simply calling the shots, ordering the days of your life in some arbitrary way. What he does with and to you is always good, even if it doesn't seem that way. The question is, do you believe that, or are you quick to question what God is doing, as if he isn't good? As if he isn't good to you?

The goodness of God doesn't guarantee ease, but it does ensure that he will not act carelessly, or out of frustration or fatigue. He is guided by his own perfect nature, and all his interactions with his people are good. He works for their good—for your good. This can be hard to see. The psalmists sometimes struggled to see what they knew to be true (see Psalm 73). The key is to look beyond what you can see with your eyes to what God has told you is true. Only then can you begin to see things as they really are, not just as they appear. You can be certain that where you find yourself right now is a part of God's good plan for you.

7

He Knows

O LORD, you have searched me
and known me!

Psalm 139:1

One of the earliest truths you learned about God was that he knows everything. He is not a God who guesses; he knows. He is *omniscient*. He knows all things that are and all things that are possible. He is unlimited in his knowledge. And yet there is a profound gospel-truth you seem to forget concerning God's knowledge. It is a truth that can steady your soul in days of turbulence and trouble. The fact that he knows all things means that he knows *you*.

This is actually one of your greatest desires. You want to be truly known—to be understood, to be seen for what you are in all your ugliness and beauty. God the Father knows you like this.

He knows your life, circumstances, fears, anxieties, doubts, and afflictions. He knows your frame and your frailty. He knows you personally. And one of the reasons this is so important is because of God's power and willingness to help his children. Yes, God is both sovereign and good, but such attributes would prove potentially disastrous to you if God did not also know you so well. He knows what you really need, not just what you ask for. He knows what will break you and what will help you. He knows what you can handle and what is too much. So when you seek God's help, power, provision, or intervention, you do not have to worry about his response. He will not get it wrong. He knows you, and therefore he knows exactly how to answer you.

This means that he will sometimes give you more than you can handle so you will be led to rely on him and his grace. Sometimes you need to be overwhelmed in order to see how dependent on grace you really are. Sometimes he will break you in order to heal you, that you might once again know how sweet his restoring grace is.

God has searched you and knows your heart. Because of this, you can rest. More than that, you can have confidence in whatever God decides to do in your life. He has taken you, your desires, your needs, and your limitations into account. Whatever has come, and whatever comes next, is not happenstance but the careful plan of the Father who knows his child better than anyone.

8

He Is Patient

But you, O Lord, are a God merciful
        and gracious,
    slow to anger and abounding in steadfast
        love and faithfulness.

Psalm 86:15

The character of God is revealed, preached, and heralded throughout Scripture. So why are you slow to hold on to it tightly? If you don't know God to be gracious, merciful, and slow to anger, you do not know his patience. And it is his patience that has led to your salvation and continues to lead you in the life of faith.

It's not that you are completely unfamiliar with the character of God. You read of it throughout Scripture and you sing of it with the church. How many thousands of ways has the Lord been good to you in this life? He has been generous toward you. He is in fact so slow to anger that you have never once faced his divine justice for even one of your sins. In all of this his love for you abounds, and he remains faithful to all the promises he made to you in his Son Jesus.

Dwell here, now. Lay hold of Psalm 86:15 and hold on tightly. The Lord is patient with you. He is not merely withholding deserved punishment, but he is giving you time to repent, to seek him in humility and faith. He is not tolerating you, but lovingly calling you to himself. And were it not for his patience, you would neither come to him nor learn from him, for even your growing in faith requires a lot of time. He is patient to teach you all you need to know. That's a good thing, since you are often slow to learn. Have you ever learned anything immediately? No, but the Lord is faithful to continually teach you, convict you, and lead you in the way.

But don't misunderstand the patience of God toward you. It is not that he simply has "a long fuse." He isn't overlooking your sin. He remains patient toward you because justice has been satisfied. God's wrath against sin is settled. Therefore his patience toward you is leading you to continue in repentance from sin and reliance on his grace. Do not ignore his patience. Do not delay in your response to his love and faithfulness. The time he has given you is time to turn to him, know him, and worship him in spirit and truth.

9

He Is Love

Anyone who does not love does not know God,
because God is love.

1 John 4:8

To say that God is love is not to romanticize his character or soften his holiness. In fact, the love of God means
very little apart from his holiness and justice. The love
of God is magnified in that he loves the unholy and
pours out blessings upon those deserving just punishment for sin.

The love of God is his effusive benevolence toward
you in Jesus Christ. It accompanies you as you walk
through your afflictions, teaching you that God has
not left you or forgotten you, nor does he intend to
hurt you. His love means that he remains ever present and intends even these difficult days for your good.
The love of God as your heavenly Father is a guardrail

that protects you from veering off the path of faith and godliness.

To say that God is love means that just as *he* is eternal and unchanging, so is his love. It does not waver, but remains constant in its perfection. You, on the other hand, grow weary of loving others, just as others grow tired of expressing love toward you. Your heart is not only small, but remains corrupt. But the Lord's love is from everlasting to everlasting.

And yet, you still doubt. Your circumstances often prompt you to ask, "Is *this* the love of God?" But be assured, it is. You can be certain of God's love, for he gave his Son up for your safety and salvation.

It is his love that gives you confidence of entering into his presence. It is his love that remembers you but forgets your sins. The love of God for his people fills heaven and earth. It is inexhaustible and incomprehensible, yet it is perfectly communicated to us in Jesus Christ.

As you persevere in faith and live as more than a conqueror of all that stands against you, the love of God will protect you. Lay hold of this love in Jesus, and rest assured that to you, the Lord himself goes by the name *Love*.

10

He Forgives

Bless the LORD, O my soul,
and all that is within me,
bless his holy name!
Bless the LORD, O my soul,
and forget not all his benefits,
who forgives all your iniquity,
who heals all your diseases,
who redeems your life from the pit,
who crowns you with steadfast
love and mercy,
who satisfies you with good
so that your youth is renewed
like the eagle's.

Psalm 103:1–5

You experience two kinds of guilt. One is the reality of your culpability before God. You have transgressed his law—you *are* guilty. The other is the sense of your corruption. You *feel* guilty. The first kind of guilt is true of you because everyone is a sinner. But not everyone knows the second kind. Until a person knows his guilt, he cannot know pardon. Until you feel the bondage of your guilt, you cannot find the freedom of forgiveness. In this sense, guilt is not your enemy.

Yes, guilt before God is the greatest problem a human being must face. That guilt will destroy you. But the sense of that guilt is itself a gift that should lead you to the only one who can deal with it. Do you see? Your guilt can ruin you, but your sense of guilt can guide you.

Your guilt before God is your own. You have no defense for your actions. There is no self-justification for your thoughts and choices. But your sense of all this should lead you not to an empty despair that ends in death, but to a hungry despair that seeks and feasts on grace!

It's good that your sins bother you. They should. They are an offense and affront to God. But your tendency to lose hope in light of them is not of faith, because faith believes and receives the pardon of God. He forgives his people. Read that again: God forgives his people. He sees your guilt, takes it from you, and gives it to his Son, who willingly received it and its punishment on your behalf. This is what it means to be saved. You have been pardoned for crimes you have committed, rescued from the justice of God to rest in the mercy of God.

Despite what so many are saying these days, you do not need to forgive yourself. You need to be forgiven. When your sins pain your heart, when the Devil accuses you of being a half-Christian whose sins are worse than anyone else's, look to the God who forgives. He has the final word on you and your guilt.

11

He Is Unchanging

For I the LORD do not change; therefore you, O children of Jacob, are not consumed.

Malachi 3:6

People often say that change is exciting. That variety is the spice of life. But the changing nature of this fallen world also brings uncertainty, fear, and suffering. Things do not remain constant. Like the apostle Paul, you have experienced both comfort and crisis. People have failed you, and you have failed others. The path you walk isn't one long, serene stroll through beautiful open fields. Your surroundings change, and the path often grows treacherous. You stumble.

But in this world of sinking sand you find the Lord, your solid Rock, unchanging in his "being, wisdom, power, holiness, justice, goodness, and truth."[1] The immutability of God is one of your great comforts, because what is true about him is always and forever true. He is always just, good, full of mercy, and committed in his love for his people. He will not break his promises to you. He will never abandon you. He will never change his mind in regard to your eternal welfare. He will never cease causing all things to work together for your good. The Lord is unchanging, and this attribute of God is what you must hold on to when walking through the valley of the shadow of death. A valley you know well.

The darkness in life is often very thick. Sometimes pain, confusion, and doubt overwhelm your spirit so that you can almost feel the darkness. It seems closer to you than God. This is when you must know, really know, the character of God. Your experience sometimes gives you the idea that God is distant, uninvolved, and uninterested. But because he does not change, you must challenge your experience with the truth. The Lord is immutable.

God will not leave you. Why? His love endures forever. Though you fall, he will not destroy you. Why? Because God remembers you and his promise to you. God will grow you in grace, strengthening your faith as you

---

[1] *Westminster Shorter Catechism*, q. 4.

walk through the dark and difficult days. You can be assured of this because he does not change. Though the world and your own heart are temperamental things, the Lord is a Rock. You can trust him.

12

He Is Jealous

> You shall not make for yourself a carved image,
> or any likeness of anything that is in heaven
> above, or that is in the earth beneath, or that
> is in the water under the earth. You shall not
> bow down to them or serve them, for I the LORD
> your God am a jealous God.
>
> **Exodus 20:4–5**

Jealousy is a word that evokes pictures of a controlling, oppressive husband who doesn't trust his spouse and denies her freedom. But the jealousy of God for his people doesn't stem from a lack of trust in his people. It comes from his desire to have an intimate and exclusive relationship with them. He calls them to maintain the fellowship they have with him above everything else.

To say that God is jealous for you is to say that he loves you, desires you, and does not want to share you with other gods. His jealousy protects you from the false gods of the world that seek to use and exploit you. His jealousy is your good.

Yes, his jealous love for you calls you to faithfulness. Does this limit your freedom? In some ways, of course it does. But why would you want to be free to dishonor the Lord? Where is the joy in finding temporal pleasure in idols that do not love you, cannot care for you, and will always hurt you?

Here is what is beautiful in God's jealousy: His love for you is fervent. His fidelity to you is unbreakable. And by his jealous love he swears to defend you and keep you. The jealousy of God for you should lift your countenance, not cast it down. You should feel safe, treasured, and compelled by his love to stay close to him. And though you fail him, he will not fail you. His love, unlike your own, is immovable.

13

He Is Listening

But know that the LORD has set apart the
godly for himself;
the LORD hears when I call to him.

Psalm 4:3

Getting the ear of someone important can be difficult. Important people are busy and have many demands on their time. Even if you get an audience with them, you may not get their undivided attention. Sometimes even those you are close to, who love you, quickly tune out in the middle of a conversation. You do it as well. If something doesn't interest you, it takes effort to stay invested in the conversation.

This somehow bleeds into your prayer life. You sometimes feel as if smaller matters don't warrant prayer. As if God were too busy to deal with your smaller issues. And when you do pray, a question lingers after you say

Amen: "Did he hear me?" But the Lord never tunes you out or wanders in his thoughts away from your prayers. The all-powerful God is all-hearing and is turned toward the needs and cries of his people. He hears. He listens. And it isn't because you're so interesting, or that your issues are greater than another's. He listens to you because of his love for you. As the God who has chosen you, saved you, and is involved in the details of your life, he knows your thoughts before you speak them. The great comfort in this is not that he simply hears you, but that you have his undivided attention.

To say that God hears the cries of his people means he is ready to answer. He is prepared to support, deliver, and lift up those who trust him. Your words, lifted to God in the name of Jesus Christ, always connect to him. So you should pray. The Lord, your God, hears both your desperate pleas for rescue and your spontaneous requests for the smaller needs in life. In all things, big and small, God is turned toward you and ready to respond. He is not at your beck and call, but he is your Father in heaven who hears and answers his children.

14

He Disciplines

My son, do not regard lightly the discipline of
the Lord,
nor be weary when reproved by him.
For the Lord disciplines the one he loves,
and chastises every son whom
he receives.

Hebrews 12:5–6

Because God loves you and is jealous for you, he will discipline you when necessary. He will bring affliction of mind, body, or circumstances to bear on your life to get your attention, confront your sinful wandering, and draw you back to himself where mercy abounds. God the Father disciplines those he loves.

This means you should be more mindful over your experiences, and your afflictions in particular. For when you suffer, you can be sure that one of two things is hap-

pening. Either God is teaching you to *rely* on his grace
and sufficiency through your pain, or he is teaching you
to *return* to his grace and sufficiency through your pain.

Nothing happens in your life apart from the good
intentions of the Lord. Nothing "just happens." God is
constantly at work in the world and your life. So even
your suffering has a design in it. At the very least you
can be certain that God is teaching you to trust him
more deeply in this season of pain. In fact, without your
current afflictions you would not learn what God wants
to teach you. But perhaps God is not only teaching you
to rely on him, but to return to him.

Are you open to the possibility that the difficulties
you face today are the result of your loving Father dis-
ciplining you for your continued and unrepentant sins?
Are you ready to receive that discipline as an act of
divine love intended to bring you back to a humble and
dependent faith? Or do you somehow believe your sins
are too small to warrant discipline?

God's fatherly love for you is too strong, and your
sins are too wicked, for you to remain undisciplined.
So use your days of difficulty to examine yourself. Ask
the Lord to help you see your corruption, that you may
repent and return to him.

Search me, O God, and know my heart!
   Try me and know my thoughts!

And see if there be any grievous way in me,
   and lead me in the way everlasting!
      (Ps. 139:23–24)

Instead of suffering fruitlessly through your trials, be sure to keep your eyes fixed on your heavenly Father who has good purposes in all you experience. Check yourself for sin that has not been dealt with. Lean on the grace and goodness of God, and you will find relief.

15

He Is Father

Our Father in heaven . . .

Matthew 6:9

When Scripture says that God is the Father of his peo-
ple, it means that you as a believer are a child of God.
He is *your* Father, and you are a part of his family.
If there was ever a doctrine that should comfort your
heart, it is that in Jesus Christ you are called a son of
God (Rom. 8:14).

All the works of your heavenly Father are honor-
able. All his actions toward you are full of grace. Like
any good father, the Lord watches over you, protects
you, and provides for you. This is comfort for the soul
that is hurting and frightened.

Your anxieties are alleviated in the fatherhood of
God. He cares for you with such love and precision
that nothing befalls you that isn't offered through his

parental purposes for your good. Remember the words of Jesus: "Are not two sparrows sold for a penny? And not one of them will fall to the ground apart from your Father. But even the hairs of your head are all numbered. Fear not, therefore; you are of more value than many sparrows" (Matt. 10:29–31).

This is gospel confidence: In Jesus Christ God welcomes you as his child, and he watches over you and cares for you with not only good intentions, but also with successful actions. He even numbers the hairs of your head. This means that no detail of your life and existence escapes God's attention, just as the life and death of each individual sparrow is accounted for in the sovereign care of the Lord. But you are no bird. You have far greater value as a person both made in God's image and adopted as a child through Jesus. The Lord is your Father, and as such his eyes are fixed on you in the midst of all you must go through.

Part 2

GOD THE SON

16

His Humanity

For there is one God, and there is one mediator
between God and men, the man Christ Jesus.

1 Timothy 2:5

Do you know the man Jesus? It makes you a little un-
comfortable to even read that, doesn't it? The *man*. You
immediately want to say, "He's fully God as well as fully
man!" Yes, indeed. But there is a kind of deficiency in
your christology that sees much of Christ's deity but little of his humanity. And if you disregard the humanity
of Jesus Christ, you will find yourself with half a Savior.

Jesus, in his humanity, experienced adversity, aban-
donment, and affliction. He knew poverty and hunger,
loneliness and betrayal, temptation and satanic attack,
divine wrath and death. The Son of God took on flesh to
experience all of this and much more, for you.

The Son could not have ransomed sinful men and

women without himself becoming one of us. To be a suitable substitute he needed to be made like us in every way (Heb. 2:17). Only "the man Christ Jesus" (1 Tim. 2:5) could fulfill the law on our behalf, take on the punishment of our sins, and rise from death for us who need life. This is why Jesus is the perfect mediator between you and your Maker.

To see the greatness of the Savior you must know both his divine nature and his human nature. The human nature of Jesus Christ shows you the depths of his love and the beauty of his humility. Do you want to see God? Look to Jesus. Do you want to see what perfected humanity looks like? Look to Jesus.

The man Christ Jesus is therefore both Savior and example. He has taken your place in his life, death, and resurrection, but he has also shown you the way of faith and godliness.

17

His Deity

For the grace of God has appeared, bringing salvation for all people, training us to renounce ungodliness and worldly passions, and to live self-controlled, upright, and godly lives in the present age, waiting for our blessed hope, the appearing of the glory of our great God and Savior Jesus Christ, who gave himself for us to redeem us from all lawlessness and to purify for himself a people for his own possession who are zealous for good works.

Titus 2:11–14

You love the idea that Jesus is the friend of sinners. You should; this is your only hope as a sinner. His grace has appeared to set the condemned free, to rescue the enslaved. You truly are saved by grace. But this Friend is not just a savior, but the *Savior*. Jesus, "our great God," has set his people free not only from sin and judgment but also from the tyranny of sin and lawless living. He is the God who gave us law and saved us from our lawbreaking so that we might become his law-keeping people.

Why did our great God appear and bring redemption? To purify for himself a people zealous for good works. You see, what makes this gospel the antithesis of other religions is not only that we are saved by God's grace alone through faith alone, but also that we are saved unto God-empowered good works over the dead works of self-powered obedience.

I know that you sometimes feel as if there is no hope for your growth in godliness. You believe that your sin will always get the better of you. But the God who saves has saved you with a purpose and a power that changes the soul and produces godliness. The God who made you a new creation will continue his work of salvation in you. Jesus has saved you and is saving you. Do you believe this?

Do you know the promises that are made to you in your great God and Savior? That he will cleanse you from your idols, put his Spirit within you, and cause you to walk in his ways (Ezek. 36:22–32)? That he prepares good works for you to walk in, and gives you grace to do so (Eph. 2:8–10)? God has not saved you and left you powerless to obey. He has saved you so that you can and will obey. Only God can do this. Religion can't do it. Commitment can't produce it. But Jesus has saved you for this purpose.

Look ahead to what lies before you, and see how God would have you live. By his grace you can do it. This isn't positive thinking, nor is it antigrace. It is resting in and acting upon the grace that Jesus Christ gives his people.

18

His Poverty

> For you know the grace of our Lord Jesus Christ, that though he was rich, yet for your sake he became poor, so that you by his poverty might become rich.

2 Corinthians 8:9

You don't know poverty—not like the truly destitute, and certainly not like your Lord Jesus Christ. His poverty was more severe than the bleakest and hardest examples you have seen. And his poverty was not the result of unrighteousness, inequality, or bad decisions. His poverty had a purpose, and he embraced it. His poverty was the means by which he would make his people rich.

You can see the poverty of Christ in his incarnation, where he laid aside the privileges of his divine nature and embraced human life. His poverty deepened in his thirst, hunger, betrayal, crucifixion, and death. And yet, the purpose of his poverty is your own spiritual prosperity. By his poverty the believer is made rich. And these riches are worth counting, and even boasting in, for they are not from you, but from the Lord. Ultimately the riches of Christ are not for you, but for him. He makes you rich so that you can display his benevolence, generosity, and grace—his glory.

Those who know the riches they have in Jesus are more able to find contentment in this life, and are moved to be more generous with what they have. So, when you find yourself discontent and miserly, consider the poverty of Jesus and the riches you have received because of it.

In Jesus you have "every spiritual blessing in the heavenly places" (Eph. 1:3). This means that you have every spiritual grace offered by God in the person of Jesus. Let me remind you of a few. In Christ you are chosen, reborn, justified, adopted, and sanctified. You are indwelled by his Spirit, protected by his power, and guaranteed to be perfected in glory. You are a member of his kingdom and an heir of the world to come. In Jesus you are perfectly and eternally loved. Christ became poor to give you all of this. What else do you need?

19

His Love

For the love of Christ controls us, because we have concluded this: that one has died for all, therefore all have died; and he died for all, that those who live might no longer live for themselves but for him who for their sake died and was raised.

2 Corinthians 5:14–15

You can see the love of God most clearly in Jesus Christ. In Jesus you see perfect love: undeserved, unrestrained, and unrelenting. It was his love that secured your salvation, and it is his love that moves you to action. Have you forgotten this love?

The love of Jesus for his people was of the highest order (John 15:13). He laid down his life for his friends—unworthy sinners who needed redemption. By his loving and sacrificial death you are rescued from sin and hell and a powerless life of futility. Do you see it? Christ died so that you might *live!* Those for whom Jesus has died are empowered to live for him instead of for themselves.

This is important because even though your heart and mind work like idol factories and you are prone to wander, you can, by God's grace, live for the glory of your Savior. The driving force behind it is the love of Jesus. It compels you. It is what will motivate you. Do you find yourself spiritually lethargic? Bored in the faith? Weak in doing what God calls you to do? Then return to the work of Jesus, to the demonstration of his divine love, and you will find that you can't help but be moved.

To be moved by the love of Jesus is not the arousing of sentimentality. It doesn't mean you merely feel something in your heart. It means that your heart and will are bound together in joy and love, producing gospel obedience (Rom. 1:5). His love influences, leads, and controls. Perhaps the simplest reason your faith is small, your love is weak, and your obedience is sparse is because you have lost sight of the love of Jesus for you.

You don't fade in your love for Christ without first forgetting his love for you (Rev. 2:4). Do not lose sight of Christ's sacrificial affection for you. It is what saved you and what will sustain you, and it will strengthen you to live for him.

20

His Temptation

Then Jesus was led up by the Spirit into the wilderness to be tempted by the devil.

Matthew 4:1

Many of your temptations are more than the subtle lure to misstep. They are often strategic and potentially deadly attacks against you. You know them, feel them, and sometimes fear them. At times you are caught flat-footed and fall almost immediately into the trap. Other times you see it coming, pray and fight against it, and escape by the smallest of margins. It hardly feels like a victory.

And then there are those times when you become frustrated by the attacks, wondering why God continues to allow them. Why doesn't he completely deliver you from them? Let me lay down a hard truth. The temptations you face today, you will face tomorrow. You are likely to face them for the rest of your life. But these temptations, as dangerous as they are, are not greater than he who is in you (1 John 4:4).

You see how Jesus was led by the Holy Spirit into the wilderness for the purpose of being tempted by the Devil? The Son of God, perfectly loved by God the Father, was led into the wilderness battleground to be assaulted by the Devil. This was not an act of cruelty on God's part; it was the means by which Jesus would begin conquering the Devil on your behalf.

What this means for you is that Jesus knows temptations. He knows *your* temptations, and has suffered them all, and far more. "For we do not have a high priest who is unable to sympathize with our weaknesses, but one who in every respect has been tempted as we are, yet without sin" (Heb. 4:15). Jesus was tempted in every way, yet he perfectly resisted. This is a key aspect of your salvation, for as the Substitute for sinners, Jesus did what you have not done. He overcame all temptation and sin on your behalf. Through faith in him your failures to resist sin are covered by his faithfulness to God. But this is not the only aspect of Christ's saving work in his temptations. He also comes to the aid of those who are tempted.

"For because he himself has suffered when tempted, he is able to help those who are being tempted"

(Heb. 2:18). Your temptations are very real, but Jesus is even more real. The flesh rages, the Devil entices, and the world lies, but Jesus reigns, he empowers, and he promises to give you the grace you need to stand up under the temptations you face.

When you are tempted, know that the Spirit is leading you into a time of testing to find strength and sufficiency in the only One who has known temptation and fully conquered it.

21

His Obedience

For as by the one man's disobedience the many were made sinners, so by the one man's obedience the many will be made righteous.

Romans 5:19

Without perfect obedience there is no hope of heaven, no peace with God. Obedience is a critical aspect of faith. God commands you to obey. He has given his law that you might know his character and ways. Yet you have been disobedient. What is your hope before God if he requires perfect righteousness? Your hope is not your own obedience, but the obedience of Jesus Christ.

Adam represented all of humanity. He was the first father—the head of the human race. But the representative rebelled. He failed in obedience, and his act of defiance against God made all humanity sinful. By nature, you are "in Adam." You have inherited from him a nature that is unrighteous and rebellious. In and of yourself you have no obedience to offer to God. But Jesus, the Second Adam, is the representative of all who believe. By faith in him you are united to a new head, and by his obedience you are counted as righteous. This is the heart of the gospel, the foundation of your relationship with God. You are saved by Jesus's perfect obedience to God the Father. Obedience matters.

But obedience is not only of interest for our justification. You have learned obedience through the gospel. God commands it, Jesus fulfills it and models it, and you learn it. As one who has been forgiven and counted as righteous, you delight in God's ways (Ps. 40:8), no longer fearing condemnation. And by faith you now obey (Rom. 1:5), however incomplete your obedience is.

It's true that your obedience is not perfect. Yet God delights in you through Jesus Christ, and he delights in your obedience through him as well (Ps. 51:16–19). Do not despair over the frailness of your obedience. God has accepted you and your works on the basis of Jesus's obedience. So rejoice and work hard, knowing that who you are and what you do are now pleasing to the Lord.

22

His Suffering

For to this you have been called, because Christ also suffered for you, leaving you an example, so that you might follow in his steps. He committed no sin, neither was deceit found in his mouth. When he was reviled, he did not revile in return; when he suffered, he did not threaten, but continued entrusting himself to him who judges justly.

1 Peter 2:21–23

Everyone experiences pain. It's not a matter of if you will suffer, but when. And then the most critical issue will be *how* you suffer. I don't mean the form your suffering will take, but the way in which you will respond to it. If your suffering is going to produce fruit and lead to peace, then your response to it must be rooted in the sufferings of Jesus.

The suffering of Jesus is unparalleled in this world. You've read detailed accounts of what he went through before and during his crucifixion. You have seen depictions of his suffering on film that have moved you to tears. You know the deepest part of his suffering wasn't physical, but spiritual, when he endured the wrath of the Father on behalf of sinners. You are saved by this reality. His suffering was for you. But Christ's suffering in your place does not save you from suffering. It rescues you from divine condemnation, but not from the world's condemnation. As a Christian you can not only expect affliction, but you can also expect a kind that is unique to the people of God. You will suffer for your faith and face many obstacles in following Jesus. And in all of your suffering you are called to look to Jesus in his suffering not only for how it saves you, but also how it guides you.

Jesus's suffering not only saves (Isaiah 53), but it also serves as an example for you to follow. When he was beaten, he did not respond in kind. When he was mocked, he didn't curse his enemies. In his most painful and isolated moments of terror he did not curse God, but trusted him. Jesus was able to see his pain in light of the justice and goodness of his Father. There was a plan, and evil would not win. Though it would cost him his life, Jesus knew that he would be victorious.

This needs to be where you go when pain floods into your life. There is no safer place than where Jesus is or has been. He has gone before you, and in fact faced much worse, and his example is one of silent submission. He voiced no selfish complaint or felt any need to justify himself. He would suffer, but God would make it right. He would die, but the Lord was bringing about a glorious deliverance—not only for the Son, but also for his people.

Your suffering is real, but those who trust the Lord will find life even in the midst of death. "Those who trust in the LORD are like Mount Zion, which cannot be moved, but abides forever" (Ps. 125:1).

23

His Death

Since therefore the children share in flesh and blood, he himself likewise partook of the same things, that through death he might destroy the one who has the power of death, that is, the devil, and deliver all those who through fear of death were subject to lifelong slavery.

Hebrews 2:14–15

Death is not only an event found at the end of a long life. You experience the daily, painful effects of death as a result of living in this fallen world. Your friends and loved ones grow weak and expire. Death sometimes comes suddenly and unexpectedly, robbing people of their dreams and desires when they lose the people they love. Death produces fear.

No one knows death better than Jesus. He knows what it is to lose a loved one to death (John 11:1–44).

He knows the fear of death (Matt. 26:39). He knows death itself, having faced it head-on, willingly, in order to save those who needed to be rescued from its dominion. But his death, as real as it was, was no defeat. Through his death he conquered the Devil, taking his power and death's sting. By the death of Jesus you are delivered, not just from the fear of death, but from death itself.

This doesn't mean that you won't taste death yourself, but that death is not the end. It does not drop the curtain on your existence, or lead to judgment. For those who believe in Christ, death becomes the means by which we enter the presence of the Lord and are set free from the frailty and frustrations of life in the flesh (2 Cor. 5:8; Phil. 1:23). Death comes for all, but the Christian does not need to fear it. Our deliverance is sure. Christ has conquered this enemy, and his victory is ours. For you, death has been made impotent. It can touch you, but cannot kill your soul. Why would you fear it?

Why should we then fear death, which is but a passage to Christ? It is but a grim sergeant that lets us into a glorious palace, that strikes off our bolts, that takes off our rags, that we may be clothed with better robes, that ends all our misery, and is the beginning of all our happiness. Why should we therefore be afraid of death? It is but a departure to a better condition.[1]

In death Jesus is your confidence and courage. There is no need to shrink back from death's presence, for the Son of God has made death the servant of the Christian.

[1] Richard Sibbes, *The Complete Works of Richard Sibbes*, ed. Alexander Balloch Grosart (Edinburgh: James Nichol; James Nisbet and Co.; W. Robertson, 1862), 1:340.

24

His Resurrection

If the Spirit of him who raised Jesus from the dead dwells in you, he who raised Christ Jesus from the dead will also give life to your mortal bodies through his Spirit who dwells in you.

Romans 8:11

Jesus's resurrection from the grave demonstrates his person and power. It proves him to be the Son of God and the conqueror of death. The Christian's redemption is completed in this great act. Jesus lived the perfect life to fulfill the demands of righteousness. He died on the cross to satisfy the demands of justice. He rose from the grave conquering the Devil and overcoming death, thus ensuring believers of a resurrection of their own. The same Spirit that raised Jesus from the dead will give life to your mortal body.

This is the great expectation of every Christian.

To die and dwell with God in heaven is glorious, but greater than that is to be raised to life with an immortal body to accompany your immortal soul, to be restored in your person fully, and in that truly glorified condition to dwell with God for all eternity. Yes, the resurrection of Jesus is the guarantee of paradise.

And yet, even now, you receive resurrection grace for this life. You have not only been crucified with Jesus, but you've been raised up in a new life with him. Your baptism points to this reality.

> Do you not know that all of us who have been baptized into Christ Jesus were baptized into his death? We were buried therefore with him by baptism into death, in order that, just as Christ was raised from the dead by the glory of the Father, we too might walk in newness of life. (Rom. 6:3–4)

"Newness of life." This is what the resurrection grants you as a believer—life that is truly alive. Your heart was cold and still, but now it beats with love for God. You have been born again, made new. It's not just that life is now worth living, but that life can now be lived.

Life has been given to you. Do not waste it. Your living, breathing, working, praying, worshiping, laughing, loving, and serving—all of it—comes through Jesus's resurrection.

25

His Reign

For he must reign until he has put all his enemies under his feet.

1 Corinthians 15:25

Jesus is not a man who lived and died. He is not even one who died and rose from the grave. He is the Lord who reigns over all creation and his church. He is high and exalted as one having all authority and power (Matt. 28:18). He reigns now from heaven and will continue to reign from his throne until his return, when your redemption will be complete and all your enemies utterly defeated.

A reigning Savior is a ruling and conquering Savior. He is a King whose kingdom has no end, whose rule is righteousness, and whose power is limitless. Jesus is the One who holds the world, your world, together. He not only oversees all that happens, but he is involved in all that comes to pass. Nothing escapes his notice, nothing evades his reach, and nothing can upset his plans. And he, your sovereign, reigning Savior, is your hope against the enemies of the world, the flesh, the Devil, and death.

In the midst of the battles raging around you and in you, you need a King with authority and power who will lead you in victory. Jesus reigns now, and will continue to do so from his throne until he comes to crush the heads of his and your enemies. This is the answer to the evil and injustice in the world that haunts your thoughts and hurts your heart. God is not sitting in heaven doing nothing. He is not merely waiting for the right time to act. He is already acting, involved, and at work. And it will all come to a glorious conclusion when Christ returns.

26

His Hold

I give them eternal life, and they will never perish, and no one will snatch them out of my hand.

John 10:28

The One who has granted you eternal life is the same One who refuses to revoke it or release it. This is your security. The Giver of the gift of life, who has all authority, holds you in his hand. This is the safest place imaginable. Who can open the hand of God? Who can snatch away what he loves and holds dear?

You have seen many people fail and fall. You have seen some lured away from the faith and others run from it in anger. You sometimes wonder about your own heart: "Will I persevere?" No doubt your weaknesses and the remaining unbelief in your own heart are serious matters. But Jesus's promise to hold you and not let go is security not only from that which is in the world, but also from that which is in your own heart. No one will snatch you away, and you cannot pry the fingers of God apart.

This is not a promise of life without wavering or wandering. You can backslide. You have before. But the good work that Jesus began in you will continue. Your faith will continue. And these things will go on not because of your commitment, but because of Jesus's faithfulness. He will not lose you. How can he? Is your heart and will that powerful? Are your sins too dangerous for him? The God who raised you up from spiritual death and gave you spiritual life will not be overcome by such things. He has you. You are his. You should find great comfort in this. Your security is out of your control and in the hands of one who never loses those who are his.

27

His Help

> We do not have a high priest who is unable to sympathize with our weaknesses, but one who in every respect has been tempted as we are, yet without sin. Let us then with confidence draw near to the throne of grace, that we may receive mercy and find grace to help in time of need.

Hebrews 4:15–16

The longer you live the life of faith, the more aware you have become of your need for grace. *More* grace. Grace to believe, fight, resist, act, and love. Jesus promises to be your help, but his help comes to those who come to him.

It is tempting to look at what lies ahead of you, what seems impossible, and to conclude with a shrug of your shoulders that God will either help or he won't, without bothering to seek his help. But he gives help to those who hold out their hands in faith. He grants wisdom to those who ask. He gives strength to those who ask. His grace, in unending measure, is available to you. Why don't you ask?

Perhaps it is because you are not looking to God when you are facing your tribulations. It's not enough to see your problem and recognize that you need help. You must not only see the danger before you (or the weakness inside you)—you must also see the Lord enthroned in grace. Then you will be moved to seek what only the Lord can provide. When your heart begins to fill with anxiety, anger, or bitterness, it is grace you need to seek.

Jesus can sympathize with you in your weakness because he knows your heart and has gone through temptation and affliction himself. And the help you receive is not from one who has learned from failure, but from victory. Jesus has been where you are, but he walked in perfect righteousness and is able to help you walk in his ways.

Draw near to the Lord by faith. Set your heart on his promises and ask for his divine assistance. You will be supplied with abundant grace in your time of need.

28

His Presence

Behold, I am with you always.

Matthew 28:20

You believe that Jesus is with you. This fundamental promise of the gospel is central to your faith and walk with the Lord. It is good to know that God is with you. It is a strengthening grace, a gift that brings confidence and courage with it. And while it is true that Jesus is with you, it is important to remember that the presence of Jesus is most powerfully experienced among his people as the church.

Jesus tells his disciples, "I am with you always" after calling them collectively to make disciples, to carry on the mission he gave the church. Jesus is saying, "Here's your calling. It is an impossible task. But fear not, for I am with you."

The presence of Jesus certainly is experienced personally, but it must not be neglected corporately. You need to take this reminder seriously. Your experience of Jesus and his presence is cut in half when you are only seeking him individually. Jesus said, "Where two or three are gathered in my name, there am I among them" (Matt. 18:20). He is present with his people. In the book of Revelation Jesus is seen as One who stands in the midst of the seven churches (Rev. 1:12–20).

If you want intimacy with Jesus, if you want to experience the blessing of his presence, you will find him among his people. The church that Jesus builds is where he delights to be. This is where his words are preached, his sacraments are administered, his people are discipled, and his glory shines. It is among his people gathered that God has historically brought revival. The outpouring of his Spirit most often comes to a people gathered.

The nearness of Jesus is a gift to you. You will find him to be close by when you read his Word and seek him in prayer. He is there to comfort, challenge, and change. But he is not only a gift to you, but to the church. To experience the fullness of the presence of Jesus you must walk with him and his church. He is never far from her.

29

His Church

I will build my church, and the gates of hell shall not prevail against it.

Matthew 16:18

Jesus's words in Matthew 16:18 are more important that you often realize. They carry a truth that is easy to miss but critical to your understanding and experience of the church.

You love the truth that *Jesus* builds the church. For all the creativity, commitment, and effort of God's people in the church, they cannot make it grow. Only the Lord gives the increase. You also take great comfort in the promise that the gates of hell, death itself, will not overcome the church. There is nothing the world or the Devil can do to destroy what God is building. But all of this is grounded upon another truth: the church is *Christ's* church.

"I will build *my* church." The church is neither the invention nor the possession of man. The church was created by, is cared for by, and is the claim of the Son of God. Until you embrace this truth, you will put too much distance between Jesus and the church, and therefore between you and the church.

You hear people say, "I love Jesus, but not the church." And though you don't say it out loud, such foolishness resides in your heart, and this creates distance between Christ and the church (at least in your mind). You avoid certain individuals for selfish reasons, and you are slow to give others a second chance because they have let you down. In truth, you look down on whole groups of people, members of Jesus's church. You think, "They aren't serious enough about theology; they are too serious about smaller issues; they don't like my tribe so I don't like them; they are doing it wrong!" However you want to paint these scenarios, the truth is you struggle with loving parts of the church.

But these are not just differing tribes in the land or different cliques in school. These men and women are a part of your family. They are members of Jesus's church. These are people whom God has loved since before creation, who have been given to Jesus by the Father, who have been purchased by Jesus through his death on the cross, and who have been united together in the Spirit.

They are just like you: made in God's image, marred by sin, forgiven in Jesus, adopted by God.

Holding indifference, apathy, or bitterness toward the church sets you against what God holds dear. It shows that what Jesus loves and saves is not worth your own time, interest, and affection. This fact applies to the church universal and the church local. God has called you to himself to be a part of his people. How you interact with the people of God reveals much about your relationship with the Lord (Matt. 25:31–46). If you love the Lord, you will love his church (1 John 4:7–12).

30

His Mission

Go therefore and make disciples of all nations.

Matthew 28:19

You like a plan and a purpose. Having a goal, a clear agenda, and an understanding of your role makes life easier. You appreciate a framework that offers clear direction and responsibilities but that also allows you to exercise freedom. Thankfully, God has not left the church to its own imagination regarding its primary purpose and role in the world (though you can't always tell by looking at a local church).

Matthew 28 provides the clearest description of the church's mission. God calls the church to *make disciples*. What does making disciples look like? Colossians 1 describes it as presenting everyone "mature in Christ" (v. 28). The church's primary mission is not renewing the city, feeding the hungry, healing the sick, or getting the right politicians in office. Of course, God does call the church to love its neighbors, which it does by feeding, healing, and working for righteousness. But the mission, the *primary interest and agenda* of the people of God, is making disciples.

If the Great Commission is making disciples, and loving your neighbor is the Great Commandment, then clearly they are connected. But they are distinct. One accompanies the other in the life of the believer and in the church, but they are not the same thing.

Christians are not alone in their responsibility to love their neighbor. Every person on earth bears this responsibility, regardless of what they believe. But it is the church exclusively that God commands to make disciples. True disciples will not neglect hospitality, generosity, service, and sacrifice as they reflect the glory and goodness of God and help the needy. But the most important need is for people to come to the knowledge of God and be transformed by the renewing of their minds.

If you can see the mission of the church clearly, you will not allow yourself to become self-centered in your spirituality. The mission is not merely to *be* a disciple, but to make disciples. This requires an outward orientation, a heart for the lost, a desire to invest in others, and a willingness to work in whatever ways God allows.

31

His Priesthood

This makes Jesus the guarantor of a better covenant . . . because he continues forever. Con-
sequently, he is able to save to the uttermost
those who draw near to God through him, since
he always lives to make intercession for them.

Hebrews 7:22–25

You need a priest. Why? Because you are not fit to stand
before God on your own. God demands purity, and you
are impure. God demands righteousness, and you are
unrighteous. God is holy, and you are unholy. Who can
ascend the hill of the Lord and draw near to God? Only
those with clean hands and pure hearts, who do not lift
up their souls to what is false (Ps. 24:3–4). And that is
not you. You need One to go before you. To stand between you and God. One who will make peace and inter-
cede on your behalf, who can show you the way to God.

All of the priests in the Old Covenant were mere shadows of the Great Priest who was to come. Those men were sinful and no better than you. They stood as priests to prepare God's people for the High Priest who would actually accomplish all that they did symbolically. The priest you need is Jesus Christ.

He is a Priest who hears your confession and forgives your sin. He is a Priest who perfects the prayers that you offer to God. And he is a Priest who continues forever. His priesthood never ends. His intercession never ceases. He does not grow old, his mind never grows dull, his love never fades. And because Jesus is your Priest forever, your access to God and your intimacy with him is forever secure.

This is reason to rejoice, to sing, and to draw near to God. You *can* ascend the hill of the Lord. You can get close without fear of judgment, for you come to him through Jesus, your High Priest. He has covered your sins, consecrated you, and introduced you to the Father. The hope of your salvation is found in the priesthood of your Savior.

32

His Kingdom

Being asked by the Pharisees when the kingdom of God would come, he answered them, "The kingdom of God is not coming in ways that can be observed, nor will they say, 'Look, here it is!' or 'There!' for behold, the kingdom of God is in the midst of you."

Luke 17:20–21

The kingdom of God is God's redemptive reign over his people and all creation. It is the spiritual realm in which Jesus is exalted as Lord and to which all Christians belong as citizens. Because Jesus is a king, there is a kingdom. This kingdom is a present reality, yet believers continue to await its full arrival. This kingdom is open to all who are willing to come in by faith in Jesus Christ. A kingdom of power and peace? Of justice and righteousness? Of forgiveness and mercy? This is a kingdom worth seeking (Matt. 6:33).

Jesus said the kingdom of God is in your midst. It is here, present and thriving. God's kingdom is now the believer's kingdom, and this present world is not to be considered your home. Sure you live here, but home is where Jesus's reign is in full effect. You live here as an alien and stranger, believing and living very differently from those around you. As a Christian you have dual citizenship, but your heart is where Christ is. His kingdom is what you continue to seek.

To seek the kingdom of God is to pursue the King by faith. When you believed in Jesus, you were immediately admitted to God's kingdom, and you are called to continue to seek his kingdom above other interests. This means you must find your identity and home there. Who you are and to whom you belong is so rooted in the kingdom of God that you will find yourself often struggling with culture shock and agony while living in this world.

Do not love this world or the things in it (1 John 2:15). Do not set your heart upon the promises this world makes, nor despair at the approaching end of this world. For Christ's kingdom is not only present, but it is also future. It will not be undone, but made glorious. What is now invisible will be made visible. This world is passing away, so live here earnestly and make the most of your time by living as a citizen of the kingdom of God, for the honor and fame of your King.

33

His Prayer

> I came from you; and they have believed that you sent me. I am praying for them. I am not praying for the world but for those whom you have given me, for they are yours.

John 17:8–9

Does the fact that Jesus prayed for you give you hope? Do you even think about it? You are always encouraged to hear that someone has prayed for you when you've been sad, frightened, or suffering. The prayers of another sinner have proved to be a blessing. How much more, then, that Jesus has prayed for you.

He even spelled it out when he prayed to the Father: "I am not praying for the world but for those whom you have given me." Jesus prayed for his people—those who believe in him. Jesus prayed for you.

Consider this for a moment. Jesus sought the will

of the Father on your behalf. The Son of God asked the Father for something. What do you think the Father's response is to the righteous request of his Son? Do you think the Father was displeased with the prayer? Did Jesus ask for something outside of the will of the Father? No! The perfect, High Priestly Prayer of Jesus was heard and answered by the Father. Jesus prayed for you, and the Father heard him. What did Jesus ask the Father?

Jesus prayed that his Holy Father would "keep them" in his name, preserving his people and their faith (John 17:11). He prayed that they would be unified, filled with joy, protected from the Devil, and sanctified in the truth. He prayed that they would behold the glory of Jesus.

He has prayed for *you*, and the Father will certainly answer. You will be kept by the power of God, you will be united with other believers, you will experience joy in the midst of sorrow, and you will have victory over the attacks of the Devil. You will be changed, and you will see Jesus. What more do you need than the surety of all this?

34

His Glory

> In their case the god of this world has blinded
> the minds of the unbelievers, to keep them
> from seeing the light of the gospel of the glory
> of Christ, who is the image of God.
>
> **2 Corinthians 4:4**

Why does the Devil not want you to see the glory of Jesus
Christ? Why is his business to blind people from behold-
ing the beauty of Jesus? It's because those who see his
glory see everything else differently than they had before. To really see Jesus—to believe—is to behold God
and be forever changed. His glory is the beauty of his
person and work. It is everything that is true about him
on display for all creation to behold. His past work as
your Substitute and his ongoing work as reigning King
show his beauty. His holiness, sovereignty, goodness,
love, and mercy show his beauty. The more you see of his

person and work, the more you behold his glory. And the glory of Jesus puts this present world in its proper place.

To behold the glory of Jesus requires a developed christology. You cannot feel your way to the glory of Jesus, for it is essentially the totality of who he is and what he has done. You must give yourself to not just knowing about him, but knowing him. And the more you know him, the less appealing the world becomes, the less painful your trials are, and the more you grow in contentment, because this glorious Christ is yours and you are his.

You want to see so much in this life. You want to see faraway countries and God's breathtaking handiwork in creation. You want to see your kids grow up into godly adults, and you want to see your spouse flourish in faith. These are all good things, but are you hungry to behold the glory of Jesus? To see that is to behold the image of God, and this doesn't inspire for a moment, but transforms you permanently. To see his glory doesn't only provide fond memories or a satisfying experience; it shapes you and fits you for eternity.

You have been made to behold and reflect the glory of your Savior. The Devil has failed in his attempt to keep you from seeing the light of the gospel, so dive deep into the truths of Jesus. Know him deeply, and share that knowledge with as many as God allows.

35

His Return

For the grace of God has appeared, bringing salvation for all people, training us to renounce ungodliness and worldly passions, and to live self-controlled, upright, and godly lives in the present age, waiting for our blessed hope, the appearing of the glory of our great God and Savior Jesus Christ.

Titus 2:11–13

With Christ's first coming he brought salvation to all who would receive him. Upon his return he will bring to his people full and final deliverance from sin and evil. In between these two events is where you live. This in-between life of grace is designed to be a life of real-world godliness and other-worldly anticipation.

The salvation Jesus brings to his people is not just the forgiveness of sins and eternal life. Through receiv-

ing these things believers are also called to lives of sacrifice, of desertion and devotion. Real-world godliness
will always require acts of desertion. In renouncing ungodliness you effectively defect from your old life, old
masters, and old ways. You give up your old idols and
commit to a new way of self-control, holy submission,
and the practice of piety. Your salvation leads you in
this new life of Spirit-empowered, grace-grounded ac-
tivity. Salvation does not leave you as a passive instru-
ment in the hands of God, but as an active participant
in the work of God.

Complementing real-world godliness is the other-
worldly anticipation of Jesus's return and the hope of
eternity—the "blessed hope." This eschatological reality should occupy a critical place in your everyday faith.
The return of Jesus is not a doctrine to be debated but
a promise to set all your hope on (1 Pet. 1:13). It is the
promise that answers the believer's greatest needs and
desires. When Christ returns, you will finally be like
him, for you will see him as he is (1 John 3:2).

Part 3

GOD THE HOLY SPIRIT

36

He Regenerates

You must be born again.

John 3:7

The world often makes a big deal out of near-death experiences. But you have experienced something far greater. You have gone from true death to true life by the Holy Spirit's work of regeneration. The Spirit's work of regeneration is the instantaneous life-giving work of renewal. You experienced this at a specific point in time—that moment when you were brought from spiritual death to spiritual life. When Jesus said one "must be born again," he implied that this is not a decision to make but a gift to receive. In fact, it is this gift, this sovereign change of your heart, that led to your faith. You believe because God made you alive by his Spirit.

Get this. God chose to give you life. This irrevocable gift of life has forever changed you. You are now a new creation, with a new heart that loves, new eyes that see, and new power that motivates what you do. That you have been born again is not merely a spiritual experience, a thing that happened and changed your perspective. It is a transformation of your soul, and because of it you are not who you once were.

One must be born again to see the kingdom of heaven. There is no sight apart from this work. There is no life apart from it. And this is why you pray to God for regeneration. This is why you can have real hope in evangelism and church growth. God grants salvation. The Spirit of God gives new life; he causes people to be born again (John 3:6–8; Titus 3:5; 1 Pet. 1:3). And since this is the sovereign working of God, something far beyond your control, you pray that he would do what only he can do.

Do you long for the salvation of your loved ones? Are you anxious about the eternal state of people you care about? Do you share the gospel with the hope that many will believe? Then you must pray for the Holy Spirit to regenerate them. By asking him to do a work that he alone can do, you move out of the realm of wishing people would believe to seeking their faith by the work of God.

37

He Indwells

And I will ask the Father, and he will give you another Helper, to be with you forever, even the Spirit of truth, whom the world cannot receive, because it neither sees him nor knows him. You know him, for he dwells with you and will be in you.

John 14:16–17

To say that the universe is vast is a gross understatement. Scientists say that just our galaxy, the Milky Way, is one hundred thousand light years across in size and contains hundreds of billions of stars and planets. Even if you could travel at the speed of light, it would take you one hundred thousand years to cross our galaxy. How many galaxies are there in the universe? Hundreds of billions. This can make you feel very small.

Then consider the God who made it all. He is not bound by time or space. He exists eternally and everywhere simultaneously. Nothing can contain him. This can make you feel even smaller. But now consider that God has spoken. He has spoken to us through the prophets and ultimately through his Son, Jesus Christ (Heb. 1:1–2). We human beings are small, and the Lord is high and exalted beyond our wildest imaginations. And yet he stoops down and takes notice of us. "What is man, that you are mindful of him?" (Ps. 8:4). Though he is highly exalted, he has condescended not only to speak to us, but also to save us from our ruin and misery. And he not only saves us, but he stays with us.

One of the great promises of the gospel is that God dwells with you and in you. The Maker of all things, whose very nature is eternal, chooses to make his home in small, finite, broken people. In you. God the Holy Spirit dwells in his people in order that his presence with them can be as intimate as possible. He is closer than you can imagine. He is present to enlighten and empower you. He is called your Helper.

As you face temptation, you must know that you do not face it alone. The same Spirit that empowered Jesus when he was tempted empowers you. He is present and powerful in you. Though you sometimes feel isolated, you are never alone. Though you know your own weakness, you are not left without power. The eternal, immortal, invisible God is with you now. Whatever comes next, you will not face it alone.

38

He Intercedes

The Spirit intercedes for the saints according to the will of God.

Romans 8:27

The longer you follow Jesus, the better you understand yourself. And one thing continues to become clearer—you are weak. You now know that you do not have the strength you once thought you had. Weakness has become painfully evident in your loving, learning, and living. You aren't incompetent or without gifts. But on your own you cannot be or do what God calls you to be or do.

So, you pray. You pray because you know you need God's grace to live, work, love, resist, overcome, and remain faithful. But even in the midst of praying you often sense your weakness. You do not know what to pray for, and you are tempted to quit. If you can't even pray, then how can you find hope and help? One of the gospel blessings of the Holy Spirit is that you never pray alone.

This is one of the fundamental works of the Holy Spirit. He intercedes for his people when they pray, and when they don't even know what to pray. What grace! What comfort to know that the Holy Spirit prays for you in your weakness. He appeals to God the Father on your behalf to gain what you need, even if you do not know what it is you lack. His prayers, always in perfect accord with the will of God, will surely be answered with a resounding, "Yes!"

Knowing that the Spirit prays for you should give you confidence in praying. For when you pray, the Spirit is with you, and when you struggle to find your way to God with feelings that cannot be expressed in coherent sentences, God still hears. He knows. And his knowledge is not based simply on his omniscience, but on the work of the Spirit who lifts you up by name to the heart of God. The Holy Spirit prays with and for you. His intercession is your assurance that God hears your heart whether you pray in words or groanings too deep for vocabulary.

39

He Fills

Do not get drunk with wine, for that is de-
bauchery, but be filled with the Spirit.

Ephesians 5:18

You long for more of God. You desire closer communica-
tion with and greater empowerment by the Lord. What
you need is the filling of the Holy Spirit. Being filled
with the Spirit is not about getting more of him, but
about being more influenced by him. You don't need
more of the Spirit, but more of his work. Filling is about
the Spirit's divine empowerment for godly living and
growing faith. Every Christian is, upon his or her con-
version, indwelled by and baptized in the Spirit. But to
be filled with the Spirit—that is your daily need.

Scripture commands you to be filled with the Spirit.
This means that Spirit-filling is something you can and
should pursue. Paul says that filling is connected with

worship, gratitude, and submission to one another in the church (Eph. 5:18–21). Don't miss that. If you want to be filled with the Spirit, you are most likely to experience it in the context of the local church.

The Spirit's work in your life will move in two directions: horizontally and vertically. Filling is connected with the worshiping saint who sees the glory of Jesus. He or she is overcome with grace that exposes and erases his or her guilt. The Spirit's filling is connected with thankfulness, for this is the humble response of a heart that has received salvation. This is the vertical direction in which the Spirit's filling moves the people of God. You are moved to worship God in humble gratitude.

The horizontal direction of the Spirit's filling directs his people to the church in service and submission to one another. Those who have been born again, those who are indwelt by the Spirit of God, love the church (1 John 4:7–21).

When the Spirit fills you, he moves you to love God as much as your brothers and sisters. When filled, you are characterized by worship, edification, and service. If you want to be filled with the Spirit, then look to the Lord in worship and look to serve your brothers and sisters. This is both the context and the consequence of Spirit-filling.

40

He Comforts

[Walk] in the fear of the Lord and in the comfort of the Holy Spirit.

Acts 9:31

You know what it is to hurt. You have experienced frustration, grief, loss, confusion, and doubt. Pain is a constant reminder than you not only live in a broken world, but that you too are broken, sinful, and in need of redemption. In this world, in your condition, you need comfort. Praise God that he has given you his Spirit, who bears the ministry of comforting the hearts of the saints.

But the Spirit's comfort isn't the slowing of your heart rate or the removal of your fears. Rather, it is the calming of your heart and guarding of your mind by means of the promises of the gospel. His comforting work is the effect of all his ministries in the life of a believer. He teaches you, leads you, revives you, grants wisdom to you, and sanctifies you.

The comfort you are promised may not be rest for the body, but it is rest for your soul. And this is good, for the deepest pains in life are not physical but spiritual. The pain for which you need the Spirit's comfort emerges from persecution, loss, confusion, doubt, and weakness. In such places you sense your helplessness and are tempted to despair. But this is where the Spirit steps in with divine comforts that no one knows but the redeemed.

One of the greatest comforts the Holy Spirit provides is the assurance that believers are indeed God's children through Jesus Christ: "The Spirit himself bears witness with our spirit that we are children of God" (Rom. 8:16). This is comfort. The surety that you belong to the Lord and he is your God is more satisfying than any other gift the world can offer. Though you may lose all you have loved in this life, you yourself will not be lost, and the Lord remains your portion forever. If you need comfort, you will find it in the gospel as the Holy Spirit applies the benefits of Christ's death and resurrection to your soul.

41

He Teaches

But the Helper, the Holy Spirit, whom the Father will send in my name, he will teach you all things and bring to your remembrance all that I have said to you.

John 14:26

You are ignorant. If you can't admit that freely and comfortably, you have some big self-awareness issues. As both a finite and fallen human being you are limited in your knowledge and in need of instruction and wisdom. How much is there to learn about God and his Word? More than your mind can even take in.

While the Lord has been kind to the church by giving us leaders who preach and teach well, he goes beyond that to supply the church, and every believer, with the Holy Spirit, who continues to teach believers what they need to know about Jesus. And this work of the Spirit isn't limited to just a few teachers within the church; this ministry is at work in all of God's people.

It's one thing to affirm that the Scripture is the Word of God, perfect and authoritative in all matters of faith and practice. But it's another thing to know that you can read it, understand it, and receive it, not only because it is clear, but also because the Spirit was given to teach you.

Is this how you read the Bible? With an eager dependency on the Spirit to teach you? Do you prayerfully open the Word not merely to deduce what it says, but to allow the Spirit to apply the Word to your heart and life in specific and needed ways? This is what he does. He teaches and reminds you of the words and work of Jesus, who took on flesh and rescued helpless sinners. But you need to be listening with expectation.

You are ignorant, but you are being taught. Pay attention. Give yourself to the Word of God in reliance on the Spirit of God, and you will know the truth of God.

42

He Leads

For all who are led by the Spirit of God are sons of God.

Romans 8:14

You are not the leader you want to be, nor are you the leader you are tempted to think you are. Even though you do lead others, you yourself need to be led. And not only by other people. You need to be led by God through the life he has set before you. The Holy Spirit will lead you, if you are willing to follow.

"Lead me" is the prayer of the people of God (Ps. 25:5). Being led by the Spirit is a sign that you are in truth one of God's children. But where does the Spirit lead his people? It's less of a geographical issue and more of a gospel issue. The Spirit leads you by helping you to understand the Word of God, by pointing you to Jesus, and by encouraging you to obey.

Being led by the Spirit is ultimately about following Jesus.

This is good news for those wandering in the wilderness. This is good news for you when you are confused or uncertain about the future. The Spirit, in conjunction with the Word, will lead you as you submit to the will and ways of God. He will prompt you to remember what is true, to trust what is real and eternal, to do what you are called to do. He will lead you by making the way of righteousness straight before you (Ps. 5:8).

The Spirit's leading is a supernatural work. He brings truth to your mind. Sometimes this is immediately profitable and pleasurable, but other times you find yourself in a difficult situation that will not yield the fruit of joy until later. Such was the case with Jesus (Luke 4:1). And remember, you are following him.

The Spirit will lead you into and through difficult days, but he will also comfort and teach you and make the way you are to go clear.

43

He Convicts

And when he comes, he will convict the world
concerning sin and righteousness and judgment.

John 16:8

You don't hate your sin enough. Your corruption doesn't
pain you the way that it should. It's easy to become
numb to your common sins and calloused even to your
more heinous acts. This is why the Holy Spirit's work of
conviction is so important to the life of faith.

His early work of conviction in your life was to bring
you to dependence on Jesus. The ongoing work of conviction serves the same purpose: to show you the danger of your waywardness and the safety of returning
to Jesus.

The Spirit doesn't convict you to beat you down,
though conviction of sin is often painful. He convicts to
show you the way to higher ground. Conviction is the

affliction of your conscience when you have been insensitive to sin, but the aim is to move you to godly sorrow and repentance. Only then do you find freedom, relief, and joy in the good news of the gospel.

Conviction makes you aware of your sin and sensitive to its danger, and therefore it makes you hungry for grace. You need conviction, because without it you tend to lean away from grace. In your work, faith, and relationship with God grace can quickly become what once was but is no more. To keep you connected to the grace of God, the Spirit pains you over your weakness so you do not forget.

When the Spirit convicts, do not turn away. Do not tell yourself that you shouldn't feel guilty. The truth is you should continually experience deliverance from guilt and your sins. Conviction is a part of that.

44

He Points to Jesus

But when the Helper comes, whom I will send to you from the Father, the Spirit of truth, who proceeds from the Father, he will bear witness about me.

John 15:26

If you really love Jesus, the way you claim to, then you will love the Holy Spirit. You will delight in him, for he points to Jesus Christ. He not only testifies of Jesus, but he points you to him in all of his work in your life.

There is no spiritual life apart from the Spirit's work. He is the one who caused you to be born again. He is the one who sanctifies you, intercedes for you, leads you, convicts you, and teaches you, and yet he does not make much of himself. He is always pointing to God the Son.

If you neglect the Spirit, you will miss the Son. And

if your love for God the Spirit does not heighten your dependence on Jesus, then it is not the Spirit at work in you. It is something else.

Jesus is what all of Scripture points to. The fullest revelation of God is in the Son. He has accomplished salvation. He has defeated the Devil. He is the One to whom you have been united. And like Scripture and God the Father, the Spirit testifies of Jesus and always leads you back to him.

What does this mean for you? It means that the more the Spirit is at work in your life, the more you will know Jesus. The more the Spirit sanctifies you, the more you will look like Jesus.

45

He Revives

Will you not revive us again,
that your people may rejoice in you?

Psalm 85:6

Do you remember when you were stronger in faith, when your heart burned hotter in love for God, when your joy of salvation was fuller? Every Christian goes through times of spiritual coldness, when it's easy to become discouraged and ask, "What's wrong with me?"

On this side of the resurrection, with all of your frailty and the sin that continues to hold on to every part of your life, you are inconsistent in your affections for God. You often need his reviving work. Praise God that he sees fit to revive his people.

Revival of the soul is not a different work of the Spirit of God. Revival is simply the work he normally does, but in greater measure. He convicts, makes alive, sanctifies, fills, and leads. This is the normative work of the Spirit in your life. Such work ebbs and flows in different seasons for different reasons, but when it ebbs, it is mostly due to your own unbelief. Impenitence, as well as neglecting the Word of God and prayer as a means of maintaining communion with God, will lead to coldness of heart and weakness of faith.

The Spirit's work of revival does not come about when God's people practice inventive or radical exercises; it comes through the normal means of grace God has given his people. Do you need God to revive your heart? Then seek the Spirit's influence. Cry out to God, store his Word in your heart, give yourself to worship, and walk in his ways. Revival is near, but you must seek it.

46

He Gives Wisdom

I do not cease to give thanks for you, remembering you in my prayers, that the God of our Lord Jesus Christ, the Father of glory, may give you the Spirit of wisdom and of revelation in the knowledge of him, having the eyes of your hearts enlightened, that you may know what is the hope to which he has called you, what are the riches of his glorious inheritance in the saints, and what is the immeasurable greatness of his power toward us who believe, according to the working of his great might.

Ephesians 1:16–19

Memorizing Scripture and knowing theology doesn't make you wise. Having knowledge is no guarantee that you will live in accordance with it. Knowledge is easy and gained through human effort. But wisdom is a gift that must be given by God.

The Holy Spirit is called the "Spirit of wisdom" because he grants to his people a deeper, experiential, and practical understanding of God's Word and the riches of the gospel (Eph. 1:17). Of all there is to know in this world, of all the mysteries and complexities of life, the knowledge of God and his ways are the most critical. This is where you need wisdom. When you are wise in the Word, you are most fit for walking in the world. The wisdom the Spirit of God gives produces peace, humility, teachability, sincerity, and good works (James 3:17). True wisdom is not mere knowledge that informs, but the application of truth that transforms.

But the impartation of wisdom is not an automatic work of the Spirit in every believer's life. It doesn't just happen. The wisdom you lack is often absent because you do not seek it (James 4:2). You are not asking for it. And when you do ask for it, you often expect it to be delivered apart from the normal means of God's operation. The Spirit will give you understanding (1:5), but it will come as you seek it in God's Word, plead for it in prayer, and are willing to receive it from brothers and sisters in Christ who speak the truth.

The wisdom you need, the wisdom the Spirit will provide, is rooted in Jesus Christ. Scripture says that he is our "wisdom from God" (1 Cor. 1:30). You know where it is to be found, and who will provide it. Will you now seek it?

47

He Sanctifies

You were washed, you were sanctified, you were justified in the name of the Lord Jesus Christ and by the Spirit of our God.

1 Corinthians 6:11

There is a great difference between personal reformation and spiritual transformation. The former is merely a choice, or a series of choices, that leads to a change in behavior. The latter is a work of the Holy Spirit in the heart of a Christian that accomplishes character change—a transformation of the soul.

The danger is that personal reformation is easy and often confused for spiritual growth. You are sometimes tempted to rest in your reformation, and even boast in it (perhaps only to yourself). But such boasting is like bragging about how well you painted your house, while the structure itself is near collapse. It might look good on the outside, but it is uninhabitable.

The Spirit sanctifies; he progressively develops your faith and godliness through your union with Jesus Christ. It is common for people to say, "I am a work in progress." This means that they are not yet what they want to be or what they should be, but that they are working on it. In a similar way all Christians are a work in progress. We are all the workmanship of God, re-created to look like our Savior and reflect his glory. As long as we are in this life, we remain that which God is continually working on.

This is good news for you when you are frustrated at what you perceive to be your slow progress in the faith. Your faith and piety appear to be so meager that they warrant no attention. Your fight against sin is often a failed attempt in battle that leaves you caring for wounds and wondering if you should enter the fray again. But the Spirit of God is at work changing you and growing you, and this transformation does not happen overnight.

Take heart, the Spirit is working in you and slowly bringing you closer to Jesus. But remember: the Spirit uses means to accomplish this work. The primary means he uses for your transformation is the Word of God (John 17:17; 2 Thess. 2:13). Your longing to look like Jesus, overcome sin, and grow in grace will always be grounded in Scripture. Stay close to the Word of God, always seeking the Spirit's help, and you will be transformed by the renewing of your mind.

48

He Grieves

And do not grieve the Holy Spirit of God, by whom you were sealed for the day of redemption. Let all bitterness and wrath and anger and clamor and slander be put away from you, along with all malice. Be kind to one another, tenderhearted, forgiving one another, as God in Christ forgave you.

Ephesians 4:30–32

When was the last time you thought about how you grieve the Holy Spirit? He laments your bitterness and anger. Your anger and harsh words affect not only the people around you but the Holy Spirit as well. By your sin, you grieve the Holy Spirit who dwells in you. Your sin defiles his habitation.

The Spirit deplores your sin but delights in your godliness. The fruit of the Spirit is love, joy, peace, patience, kindness, goodness, faithfulness, gentleness, and self control. Your soul is designed to be a garden of sorts, one that bears fruit for him who tends it.

Do not grieve the Spirit by your persistent sin, but honor the Spirit by cultivating godliness. Unrepentant sin works against his gardening; it is a sowing of weeds where he is at work to make things beautiful. The quickest way to stop grieving the Spirit is to be a person of repentance. Your ground-level garden work is to uproot the weeds of unrighteousness through confession and consecration. By turning from sin and drawing near to Jesus Christ you are watering the soul and seeding it with the Word of God.

Do not grieve the Spirit, but gladden his heart with the fruit he produces. It is a harvest that is enjoyed by him, yourself, and others around you.

49

He Gives Gifts

Now there are varieties of gifts, but the same
Spirit; and there are varieties of service, but the
same Lord; and there are varieties of activities,
but it is the same God who empowers them all
in everyone. To each is given the manifestation
of the Spirit for the common good.

1 Corinthians 12:4–7

You are not *gifted* in the way most people think when
they hear that word. On your good days you feel pretty
average. On bad days you feel pretty worthless. But
know this: the Holy Spirit has given you gifts to use
for God's glory and the church's good. You are far more
useful than you can imagine.

Do not let your thoughts of spiritual gifts run immediately to the debates about cessationism and continu-
ationism. Though that is certainly an issue to work out

with Scripture, you need to understand this work of the Spirit in your own life.

You have been created in Christ Jesus for good works. The Spirit not only sanctifies you and leads you in those works, but has gifted you in particular ways that suits you for ministry and service to and through the local church. What grace! Your spiritual gifts are gifts upon gifts in the salvation you have from the Lord. The Father gave you Jesus, Jesus gave you eternal life, and together they have given you the Holy Spirit. And the Holy Spirit has given you spiritual gifts.

You have received much, and much is expected of you. As you have received, you now must give; you must share out of your abundance. You think of this in financial terms, but the most common and fruitful form of your giving will be of a more spiritual nature.

Do you know how you have been gifted? Are you using your gifts? Cultivating them? Or are you hoarding them, keeping them all to yourself? When you feel useless and become inactive, you are withholding from others what God expects you to distribute freely. You have been given, and should be giving of yourself freely.

50

He Resurrects

If the Spirit of him who raised Jesus from the
dead dwells in you, he who raised Christ Jesus
from the dead will also give life to your mortal
bodies through his Spirit who dwells in you.

Romans 8:11

The great hope of the Christian is not heaven, which
is often conceived of as a disembodied existence in the
spiritual realm. The great hope of the Christian is the
resurrection. The same Spirit who raised Jesus from
the dead will raise his people in glorified bodies to
dwell with God in paradise for eternity. You are made
for that kind of existence. Body and soul. To breathe,
taste, touch, work, play, and rest before the face of God.
Death and frailty mar your physical life now, but there
will be a day when life is fully restored.

This is important for you, the church, and all creation, for it is the final deliverance from death and sin. It is a return to paradise, but a paradise that is far better than the garden of Eden. The Devil will be vanquished, death will be cast into hell, and righteousness will reign.

The Spirit's presence in your life now is the promise of that future resurrection. His presence in you now also demonstrates his resurrection power in smaller measure through the impartation of power. You can experience the "power of the resurrection," but it now comes in conjunction with the fellowship of Christ's sufferings (Phil. 3:10). The power of the resurrection is in you now to kill sin, live unto God, and bear witness of Jesus Christ.

You taste of the resurrection now. And its future arrival is when all that you have experienced of the Spirit so far will be brought to the fullest measure. It is coming. Look ahead, and live for that day.

Also Available from Joe Thorn

"After reading *Note to Self*, you will not only have Joe's notes on how to preach to yourself on issues related to God, others, and yourself, but also you will have a model for practicing the discipline on your own."

ED STETZER, President, LifeWay Research

"*Note to Self* is a gospel-guided smart bomb scoring a direct hit on our strongholds of emptiness. But the explosion it detonates is life giving. It clears the way for Christ to enter in with powers of salvation where we really need help."

RAY ORTLUND, Lead Pastor, Immanuel Church, Nashville, Tennessee